THE LIFE
AND PRAYERS OF
SAINT JUDE

Lex...
Enjoy this book.
Know your St Jude's
life & let him
inspire you.
Love
Patri & Lola

About Wyatt North Publishing

Starting out with just one writer, Wyatt North Publishing has expanded to include writers from across the country. Our writers include college professors, religious theologians, and historians.

Wyatt North Publishing provides high quality, perfectly formatted, original books.

Send us an email and we will personally respond with 24 hours! As a boutique publishing company we put our readers first and never respond with canned or automated emails. Send us an email at hello@WyattNorth.com, and you can visit us at www.WyattNorth.com.

Foreword

Also known as Saint Jude Thaddeous, Saint Jude is known as the most powerful Patron Saint of Desperate Cases. Christians turn to Saint Jude for hope in what often seem like hopeless circumstances.

Whether it an illness in the family, a dissolving marriage, or financial struggles, Saint Jude answers our calls when we are at our darkest hour.

God rewarded Saint Jude with the incredible power to help the desperate. Saint Jude is a true friend, who we can look to when feeling hopeless and alone.

During a time in our world when resources are few and families find themselves in desperate times, calls to Saint Jude are louder than ever.

Table of Contents

Quick Facts

The new "Quick Facts" section in **The Life and Prayers** collection provides the reader with a collection of facts about each saint!

Born:

1st century AD, Roman Province of Galilee

Died:

1st century AD, Roman Province of Syria

Feast:

October 28 (Western Christianity)
June 19 (Eastern Christianity)

Attributes:

Axe, club, boat, oar, medallion

The Life of Saint Jude

An Introduction to His Life

The Apostle, Saint Jude Thaddeus, is known as the most powerful Patron Saint of Desperate Cases. Not to be confused with Judas Iscariot, another disciple, and the betrayer of Jesus, Saint Jude is sometimes referred to as "the brother of Jesus."

Christian individuals turn to Saint Jude for hope in what often seem like hopeless circumstances. Whether it an illness in the family, a dissolving marriage, or financial struggles, Saint Jude answers our calls when we are at our darkest hour.

God rewarded Saint Jude with the incredible power to help the desperate. Saint Jude is a true friend, who we can look to when feeling hopeless and alone.

During a time in our world when resources are few and families find themselves in desperate times, calls to Saint Jude are louder than ever.

The tradition and life of Saint Jude is more than just a story in history. Saint Jude's life and devotion reflect a great power among all Christians. This is the power to overcome obstacles and times that seem hopeless. Christians can turn to faith to triumph impossible odds and find light in the darkest of places.

To explore the life of Saint Jude, we can turn to the Gospel, Narratio de Imagine Edessena, the writings of Eusebius, The Contendings of the Apostles, The Golden Legend, The Doctrine of Addai, Acts of Thaddaeus, and many other helpful sources.

The Early Life of Saint Jude

There is quite a dearth of information regarding the early life of Jude. Nevertheless, the various sources provide only a few tidbits about his early life. Jude tells his audience when he is preaching to them in Edessa that he is originally from the city Paneas, later named Caesarea Philippi, located along the Jordan River. This may have been the city of Jude's birth, since the gospel of Matthew (13:55) suggests that he grew up in Nazareth, since the locals know him and his family by name.

So it was there, in Paneas, that Cleophas and Mary (of Cleophas) gave birth to two of the Church's most prominent saints, James and Jude. As a young man, Jude married a woman named Mary and they had at least one child together. His wife and child/children are mysteriously absent from any of the stories of his later life.

Some scholars speculate that his wife may have been one of the women mentioned in connection with Jesus' ministry at various points in the Gospels, but nothing definitive is known.

A strict biographical book about Saint Jude would be short indeed. Instead, below the reader will find an outline of stories that makeup the life of Saint Jude.

Saint Jude and Ananias

The story of Saint Jude and Ananias appears in the <u>Narratio de Imagine Edessena</u>, which is often attributed to Constantine Porphyrogenitus. describe a wonderful story of Jesus, with some foreshadowing imagery of Jude's attempts to spread the word of his miracles.

As the story goes, one day while Jude was listening to Jesus' teaching and watching him perform his many miracles, a letter carrier from Syria named Ananias was passing through on his way to Egypt. Ananias took note of Jesus and his disciples and the wonderful work in which they were engaged, but he knew he would be getting himself into trouble if he stayed to investigate further when he was supposed to be delivering a message to Egypt. So Ananias asked Jude briefly about Jesus' ministry and where he might find them in the coming months. Jude answered his questions and Ananias continued on his journey to Egypt.

It wasn't until a few months later that Jude saw Ananias again. The latter had completed his mission to Egypt and now was 'off the clock.' He could converse much more freely with Jude without interfering with his work. Ananias had seen in Jesus the possibility of his own career advancement. His king, Abgar, whom he served, was a very sick man and his present quality of life was very poor. Ananias asked Jude at length about the types of diseases that Jesus had healed, and watched Jesus heal others with his own eyes. Once he was convinced that Jesus was the real deal and not a sham, he said good day to his new friend Jude and enquired again as to their whereabouts in the coming months.

Months passed and Jude gave little thought to his newfound friend from the north. During those months, back in Edessa, Ananias had approached King Abgar with news of Jesus, his healing ministry and also the Jews who opposed him. When Abgar heard about the way the Jews had been treating Jesus and their plots against him, he called for his army to be assembled so that they could destroy the Jews who opposed Jesus. His advisor quickly pulled him aside and reminded him gently that they were now under Roman rule and he had signed a peace treaty with Emperor Tiberius that would forbid any such action. Abgar was frustrated, but knew that his initial instinct was rash and that his advisor was right. He spent some time formulating a new plan, bouncing it off his various advisors, before he decided on the best course of action. He would write a letter to this Jesus and send it with Ananias asking for Jesus to come to Syria. Because Ananias was well-known for his skill in painting, he would also ask Ananias to paint a likeness of Jesus in case he was delayed.

Back in Jerusalem, Jude was listening to Jesus teach the large crowd assembled before him, when Jesus turned to Thomas alerting him of a man sitting at on a rock outcrop several yards off holding a parchment and some paints. He asked Thomas to fetch the man and bring him forward. Jude recognized his friend and watched intently as Thomas led him before Jesus.

Jesus wasted no time and said, "Greetings Ananias. You have no need to paint my image on a parchment. My Father has already revealed to me both the purpose of your visit and the contents of the letter you carry from your master, King Abgar. Do not be afraid. My Father is panged by the leprosy and chronic arthritis that Abgar has endured for years which have been causing excruciating pain in his joints. A king such as Abgar should not be forced to spend most of his time in bed and to turn away even his closest friends from seeing him. Your master has shown true faith. Having said that, may I see the letter, all the same?"

Abgar stood astonished by the words Jesus had spoken to him. He then approached Jesus humbly and handed him the following letter:

> Abgar Uchama the Toptarch to Jesus, who has appeared as a gracious saviour in the region of Jerusalem—greeting.
>
> I have heard about you and about the cures you perform without drugs or herbs. If report is true, you make the blind see again and the lame walk about; you cleanse lepers, expel unclean spirits and demons, cure those suffering from chronic and painful diseases, and raise the dead. When I heard all this about you, I concluded that one of two things must be true—either you are God and came down from heaven to do these things, or you are God's Son doing them. Accordingly, I am writing to beg you to come to me, whatever the inconvenience, and cure the disorder from which I suffer. I may add that I understand the Jews are treating you with contempt and desire to injure you: my city is very small, but highly esteemed, adequate for both of us. (Eusebius, *History of the Church*, trans. G. A. Williamson, 1989, I.13)

Upon reading the letter, Jesus asked Ananias for a bit of papyrus and a writing tool and composed the following reply:

> Happy are you who believed in me without having seen me! For it is written of me that those who have seen me will not believe in me, and that those who have not seen will believe and live. As to your request that I should come to you, I must complete all that I was sent to do here, and on completing it must at once be taken up to the One who sent me. When I have been taken up I will send you one of my disciples to cure your disorder and bring life to you and those with you. (Eusebius, *History of the Church*, trans. G. A. Williamson, 1989, I.13)

Jesus finished writing and handed Ananias the letter, but the look on Ananias' face said it all. Jesus had already done more than custom would permit him to ask. What could he do about his master's request for a likeness of Jesus' face? Jesus perceived the problem without any words being spoken and found a basin of water nearby and washed his face. A disciple then handed him a towel, with which to dry off. But instead of wiping his face in the usual manner, he pressed his face into the cloth in a profound way that imprinted his image upon the cloth.

When he removed the cloth from his face, he gave it to Ananias with instructions that Abgar could use this as a minor comfort for his sickness until the time that one of his disciples could arrive and cure him.

Saint Jude and Saint Peter in Syria

The story of Saint Jude and Saint Peter in Syria is based on The Contendings of the Apostles. The story of Jude and Peter's travels provides us with a glimpse into their work to spread Christianity following Jesus' resurrection.

After Jesus' resurrection, Peter and Paul appointed various apostles to minister different regions of the Greco-Roman world. Thomas remembered Jesus' promise to send a disciple to Abgar, and recommended that Paul appoint Jude to the region of Syria because of the friendship Jude had developed with Ananias. Paul agreed and appointed Jude as an apostle to Syria.

Jude was cautious by the prospect of leaving Palestine and asked his friend Peter to accompany him initially on his journey to Syria until he had a chance to get settled. Peter had no sooner expressed his willingness to accompany his friend than the risen Christ appeared before them both. He spoke words of comfort and solace to Jude and affirmed the divine mandate behind this journey. Then the risen Christ ascended back to heaven while they looked on.

They packed their few belongings and set out northeast on the three-week long trip from the Mount of Olives to Edessa. As they approached Syria, Jude was still anxious about what time in Syria would hold for him and he expressed his desire for foreknowledge to Peter. Peter devised a plan to discern the general will of God concerning their time in Syria. They were passing an elderly farmer, who was in the midst of plowing his field. Peter explained to Jude that he would approach the farmer and ask for some food. If the farmer offered them food, this would be a good omen; but if he claimed to be without food, they should interpret that as a bad omen.

After he had sufficiently explained his plan to Jude, Peter approached the farmer and politely asked his portentous question. The farmer explained to Peter that he did not have any food out in the field with him while he was working, but that if Peter would be willing to stay with his oxen to prevent them from dragging the plow aimlessly through his field it would give him the opportunity to return to his house and fetch some food for the two of them. Peter promptly agreed to the elderly man's request and further enquired as to whether the farmer owned the field in which they were standing and these oxen, which he would be watching. The farmer replied that he owned the field outright, but was only renting the oxen. With that the farmer returned to his house, leaving Peter and Jude with the oxen.

Once the farmer had left them, Peter realized that his scheme to determine the general will of God for their trip would cost the elderly man precious daylight in which to complete his plowing. Therefore, Peter conferred with Jude and decided that the best course of action would be to continue plowing the field himself while the farmer was preparing their lunch. While Peter prepared himself for this task, Jude objected to Peter's decision on several counts. He noted that Peter was quite advanced in age himself and more importantly, that he was now responsible for the entire Church and would be foolish to risk his own well being performing manual labor.

Peter relented to Jude's persuasive arguments and allowed Jude to take the plough from him and perform the work. By the time the elderly farmer returned from his house with their lunch, not only had Jude plowed an additional thirty furrows for the farmer, but in response to the prayer's of these two apostles for God's blessings on these fields, God had caused not only the seeds to fully sprout, but the ears had become full of grain as if it were harvest season already. He stood dumbfounded by the work of God that the apostles had performed in his midst. Immediately he asked them who they were and where they had come from. Falling on his face before them the elderly farmer declared his intention to follow them, believing that they were gods.

Peter corrected the man, bringing him to his feet and explained that they were indeed mortal and not gods. He explained to the farmer that they were apostles of Christ Jesus who had taught them spiritual truths and had now sent them out into the world so they might teach others the necessity and means for repenting their sins and inheriting eternal life. The farmer asked Peter what was needed for him to inherit eternal life. Peter engages in something called *midrash* in Jewish circles, which was a common method the early church used for interpreting the Old Testament.

Recalling the exchange between Jesus and the lawyer recounted in the Gospel of Luke (10:25-28), Peter quoted the statement (Deut. 6:5) that immediately follows the *shema* (Deut. 6:4), which is the closest thing to a Jewish creedal statement. Peter then asked the elderly man if he was either a husband or a father. When the man affirmed that he was both, Peter continued by citing the sixth and seventh of the Ten Commandments (prohibitions against murder and adultery) to which he appended another prohibition (against lying under oath) from Leviticus (19:12).

So far in this exchange Peter acted as one might more or less expect. The next statement out of Peter's mouth though comes as somewhat of a shock to those intimately familiar with the New Testament. He continues, "What thou dost not wish men to do unto thee, that thou shalt not do unto men." This negative corollary of the Golden Rule (Luke 6:31) that appears in similar form in Tobit (1:16; Greek 1:15) may have been the basis for Jesus' positive formulation.

Grateful that Peter (and Jude) had given him the keys to eternal life, the elderly farmer asked whether he may in any way repay the two for their kindness indicating that he was willing to leave his fields to follow the two apostles. Peter reassured the man that he was not in their debt, but indicated that they would appreciate a home-cooked meal from his wife. He also indicated to the elderly farmer that they are in no rush, and the farmer should feel free to return his rented oxen before their evening meal. Delighted that he could at least show some hospitality to the apostles, the old man gathered the oxen, plucked a ripe piece of corn from the field and headed for town.

As he navigated his way through the throngs of people gathered at the city gate, which functioned as the center of trade, commerce and gossip during the ancient period, a few other farmers took notice of the ear of grain he carried in his hand. These farmers were taken aback after seeing the ear of corn. They had been tirelessly sowing their cornfields for the past several weeks and would not expect to harvest corn for another five to six months.

One of the farmers asked the old farmer to disclose the origin of the ear of corn he was carrying so nonchalantly. But the old farmer did not even acknowledge the question he was being asked. He continued on through the city gates towards the ranch where he had rented his oxen. By evening the man had returned the oxen and was enjoying a wonderful home-cooked meal with his wife and his new found friends, the apostles.

Meanwhile, the flummoxed, and ignored, farmers tracked down the local Roman judges and ratted out the old farmer with his mysterious ripe ear of corn. The Roman judges were not content to allow trickery in their city and investigated the matter by sending a messenger to the old man's house.

A messenger arrived the following morning, and told the old man that the Roman judges were not only demanding that he explain himself to them, but under penalty of painful death. In his newfound excitement, the elderly farmer triumphantly declared, "I do not fear death, because I have found life."

Nonetheless, he related the entire story to them of how he met the apostles and the miraculous things they accomplished in his presence. The Roman judges later demanded that the old man to fetch the apostles for them. But the farmer suggested that since the apostles were staying with him, that the easier course would be for the judges to come to see the apostles at his house.

The judges conspired as to the best course of action. They were convinced that these two tricksters were among the twelve 'sorcerers' who were rumored to be travelling throughout the region. While some of the judges wanted to kill these 'sorcerers' straight away, others objected that based upon the rumors they had heard, these 'sorcerers' would be capable of calling down fire from heaven or even a flood to destroy them if they attempted anything of the sort. So they concocted a new plan. Based on the rumors, they knew that these sorcerers hated 'fornicators.' They determined they would find a prostitute and convince her with bribes or threats to stand at the city gates entirely nude. By this means, the judges would prevent these 'sorcerers' from even entering their city.

The judge's plan was in place. When the apostles came to the city gates and saw the woman, she confessed to them her immoral lifestyle as she had been prompted to do. The two apostles immediately began to pray, but it was Jude's bold and specific prayer to which the Lord inclined.

Jude prayed, "O my Lord Jesus Christ, I ask you to send Michael the archangel, so that he might suspend this woman in mid-air by the hair of her head until we have entered the city. When we want to leave then bring her down again." Jude was quite familiar with the archangel

Michael and what he could do, since he referenced Michael and his struggle with Satan over the body of Moses in his epistle (Jude 9).

The Roman judges had hid themselves at a distance so that they might watch how their plan unraveled. They looked on in astonishment as the naked woman was lifted off the ground, but they could not see the archangel Michael holding her by the hair. At the same time the prostitute began screaming hysterically. She began identifying all her 'Johns' from the city by name, pleading for them to repent and appeal to the apostles to show mercy on her. But her pleas fell on deaf ears because Satan had stopped them up and hardened the hearts of the men in that city.

The apostles discerned the presence of the enemy and they raised their voices together in prayer to God for the men of the city. While the apostles prayed, Michael lowered the woman and then went throughout the city exorcising the evil spirits that had gained a foothold there. Once Michael had laid the groundwork, Peter and Jude were then able to travel throughout the city preaching the gospel of Jesus Christ, converting the whole city. They held a mass baptism for all the new believers in the city and appointed bishops and priests to act as local church leaders. They even appointed the former prostitute as a minister in the church. Peter and Jude remained in the city for weeks healing the sick, giving sight to the blind, speech to the dumb and hearing to the deaf. They cast out demons, made the lame walk and even raised the dead.

As they continued to minister in that city, a rich young man approached and bowed low before them while they were in the marketplace. Like the old farmer before him, he too asked the apostles what he must do in order to inherit eternal life. Peter answered this young man the same way he had answered the poor farmer. When Peter asked the young man about his marital status, the young man confided not only that he was a bachelor, but that as such he had amassed a good deal of wealth as a carpenter. Upon learning this, Peter instructed the rich young man to distribute the entirety of his possessions to the poor.

Peter had not realized that this man had a quick temper, which flared up upon hearing Peter's advice causing him to jump on top of Jude in an attempt to strangle the life out of him. Trying to calm himself down, he eased his hold on Jude slightly asking if he too had similar advice. Despite the obvious implied threat, Jude explained that they had faced a similar situation while they accompanied Jesus and that Jesus had told that man that it would be easier for a camel to go through the eye of a needle than for a rich man to enter the kingdom of heaven. This answer clearly did nothing to appease the anger of the young man, who became all the more furious as he began to wring Jude's neck. Seeing the peril Jude was in, Peter implored the man to stop choking Jude, offering to show him a demonstration of the truth of Jesus' words.

This must have intrigued the rich young man who reluctantly released his vice-like grip on Jude. While Jude was catching his breath, Peter stopped a man walking through the marketplace with a camel and asked him to help with their brief demonstration. The camel owner was in no real rush, and was curious what this demonstration would entail.

Now that Jude could finally breathe again, he and Peter found the booth with the sewing equipment and asked the proprietor if they could borrow a needle for their demonstration. Never one to pass up the opportunity for more sales exposure, the proprietor handed the apostles his best selling needle with a large eye. But Peter returned it to him, blessed him, and this time specified that for his demonstration he wanted the needle with the smallest eye in the man's booth.

A crowd had gathered and Peter and Jude were in possession of both the camel and the needle, they stood on a crate in the marketplace raising their hands to heaven and prayed.

> O Lord Jesus Christ, to whom belongs the power over all things, we ask that you listen to our request and prayer, to demonstrate your power, in order that these people will know that everything you say is true. O Lord, listen to the prayer of your servants. Look, you see what it is your apostles desire to do, be pleased then that this camel may enter through the eye of this needle, and I will praise your name.

When they finished praying, Peter turned to the owner of the camel and said to him, "In the name of our Lord Jesus Christ, enter in through the eye of this needle, you and your camel."

Just then the man along with his camel walked through the eye of that needle. The crowd was in awe, but just in case any of the onlookers had missed it or doubted what they saw he had the man walk through a second time. The crowd responded with this creed, "There is no god save the Lord God of these two apostles, Peter and Jude."

But the reaction was not limited to the crowd. The short-tempered young man who had only moments before been wringing Jude's neck, tore his clothes hitting himself in the face while he bemoaned how he had treated Jude, who he now recognized as a righteous man.

He bowed low before them crying bitterly. He acknowledged his former selfishness and greed asking for the apostles to divvy up all his possessions among the poor and needy so that God might forgive him. They taught him a short catechism and baptized him and he joined the ranks of the newly formed local church.

Before leaving the city, Peter and Jude built a church for the people and taught them the sacraments. They also copied several books from the Old and New Testaments to keep them grounded in the faith.

Saint Jude and Saint Peter in Persia

The story of Saint Jude and Saint Peter in Persia appears in <u>The Golden Legend</u>, providing additional examples of Jude's incredible life and miracles.

Peter and Jude took a detour to Persia before travelling to the Syrian capital of Edessa. In one of the cities in Persia they entered there was a military commander from Babylon named Baradach, who was preparing to go to battle, but who had been unable to get a clear answer from his diviners concerning the outcome.

When Baradach asked his diviners for the reason an answer was not forthcoming from the gods, they replied that the gods must have shut their mouths because of the apostles who had arrived in the city. Incensed at this delay, Baradach found the apostles and asked them who they were and what they were doing in this city. Jude and Peter answered Baradach that they were Hebrews and servants of Jesus Christ and had come for his well-being.

Baradach told the apostles that he did not have time for them as he had a battle that needed attending. In response, the apostles told Baradach that they could introduce him to the one who could both give him victory over the rebels and appease their demands. Taken aback by their words, Baradach declared sarcastically that they must be more powerful than his Babylonian gods, who had been unable to predict the outcome for this battle. He then asked if Peter and Jude would be willing to predict the battle's end.

Quick-witted as usual, Peter turned Baradach's sarcasm on its head, saying, "Well since you know your gods are liars, our one condition is that they predict the outcome of the battle that they have so far been so reluctant to do. Otherwise, there will be no way for us to prove they have lied to you."

Baradach saw no downside to the challenge from these foreigners and demanded an answer from his diviners. They consulted their gods, predicting that it would be a massive battle producing many casualties on both sides. The apostles let out a guffaw upon hearing the advice of the diviners. Baradach was not amused and looking at Peter and Jude said, "I am standing here trembling while you laugh!" Jude then said to Baradach, "Without a doubt, you will be at peace. Tomorrow morning the Medes will come in the third hour and they will surrender before your power in peace."

Now it was the diviner's turn to laugh. Looking at Baradach they said, "These foreigners are trying to trick you. While you are waiting here on their advice, your enemies will come and vanquish you." The two apostles clarified the matter for Baradach, "We are not asking you to wait here for a month, but only for one day and you will be victorious in peace."

Baradach had heard enough of the back and forth between the opposing religious emissaries and ensured that both parties agreed that whomever was proved correct would be honored and whomever was proved a liar would be punished. Both parties agreed to these terms and then waited for the outcome. They did not have long to wait, because the next morning the events transpired just as Peter and Jude had prophesied through the Holy Spirit that they would.

Baradach then summoned the diviners and ordered them burned for heresy and their belongings given to the apostles. But Peter and John both quickly raised their voices in protest in hopes that Baradach might spare the diviners. They explained that the purpose of their visit was not to slay the living, but rather to raise the dead. They also would not take any of the diviners' belongings.

Baradach could not believe his ears. He] ushered Peter and Jude into the presence of the king declaring that they must be gods in the form of men. When the palace sorcerers heard what Baradach said about the apostles, they became jealous and accused them of plotting against the king and his territory. But having seen what the apostles did with respect to his diviner's, Baradach quickly invited the palace sorcerers to set up their own challenge with Peter and Jude. The sorcerers had a multitude of tricks up their sleeve and immediately decided upon their favorite. They asked Baradack to bring eloquent lawyers and philosophers before them known to be able to speak at length at a moments notice. Then the sorcerers explained that they would make anyone who stood before them dumb. The lawyers and philosophers were brought before the palace sorcerers and it happened just as they had predicted. They explained that they would return their speech, but remove their sight making them blind. Once again, they were able to perform the feat just as they had predicted.

Baradach brought the lawyers and philosophers blind and confused before Peter and Jude. Peter opened their eyes and asked them to worship the one true God. He and Jude then made the sign of the cross appear on each of their foreheads. They were then sent before the king and the palace sorcerers a second time. This time the lawyers and philosophers spoke eloquently against their sorcerers belittling them in front of the king. Humiliated, the sorcerers became angry and conjured up a large number of serpents. The frightened king summoned the apostles.

Peter and Jude reentered the throne room, filled their coats with the serpents and threw them at the sorcerers. At the same moment they commanded the sorcerers not to move in the name of the Lord Jesus, but to scream and cry out in pain in order to demonstrate how much pain the serpents, which they had created, were inflicting. At that moment the palace sorcerers stood dead in their tracks screaming and howling at the top of their lungs as the serpents ripped chunks of flesh from their bodies.

The king told the apostles to let these sorcerers die along with the serpents. To this Jude answered in the same manner that Peter had earlier that their mission here was to raise the dead, not to kill the living. Jude continued with a prayer to the living God and commanded the serpents to suck back the venom they had injected into their victims and to return to the hell from which they came. But this last action the serpents performed of sucking out their venom inflicted more pain on the sorcerers than they had suffered from the initial bites and the screaming was prolonged for some time. When the serpents were no more and the screaming had subsided, Peter and Jude both looked at the sorcerers and said, "You will suffer with this excruciating pain for three days, but on the third day you will be well again."

The sorcerers remained in this state of severe pain for three days unable to eat or drink or sleep. The apostles had hoped that this would be the lesson that would cause them to repent, but as soon as they were healed they fled from the apostles to find another palace wherein to practice their sorcery.

* * *

While Peter and Jude were in that region, the daughter of a high-ranking official had become pregnant out of wedlock. During the course of her pregnancy she would not divulge the name of the father. But through the pain of delivery, she pronounced the name of one of the prominent deacons as the father of her child. Upon hearing this, her close friends were ready to kill the deacon for his crime. But word of the situation had reached Peter and Jude, who came to investigate the matter more thoroughly.

They asked the midwife when the child was born and the midwife informed them that the child had been born the previous day in the first hour of the day. The apostles then asked that both the daughter and the deacon be brought before them.

Peter looked the woman in the eyes and asked her to swear in Jesus' name whether the deacon was indeed the father of her child. The woman then answered Peter honestly and confessed that the deacon was chaste and a holy man and that he had never done such a thing to her. The woman's high-ranking father and his wife pleaded with Peter and Jude to press their daughter further and to reveal the real father so that he could be brought to justice. But Jude explained to him that they were primarily concerned in saving innocent lives.

Saint Jude made it his mission to protect, rather than punish. On another occasion there were two cruel tigers that had escaped from the pit in which their owner kept them. They had been creating havoc throughout the region devouring anyone whom they encountered. Peter and James found the tigers and tamed them in the name of Jesus so that they were no more dangerous than a lamb. Indeed, Saint Jude did not strike down the beasts, he civilized to protect the people of the world.

After these events Peter and Jude remained in Persia for a year and three months. During this time, they baptized the Persian king and more than sixty thousand men.

Saint Jude and King Abgar

Based on <u>The Doctrine of Addai,</u> the story of Saint Jude and King Adgar starts off when Peter and Jude separate. Jude continues his pilgrimage spreading God's word and his miracles to men of great power.

After their trip to Persia, Jude said farewell to Peter and travelled on to Edessa. When he arrived he met a man named Tobias who invited him to stay in his house. Word quickly spread through the region concerning Jude and the mighty works he was performing.

When word reached a servant of the king, Abdu, he remembered the words from Jesus' letter to King Abgar that had been read in his presence many times, "When I have been taken up I will send you one of my disciples to cure your disorder..."

Although he loved his king and wanted very much to see him made well again, Abdu himself suffered from a severe case of gout in his feet. If a healer was visiting the palace, he just might address Abdu's medical condition as well.

Abdu excitedly reported to Abgar that based on the reports he was hearing, he believed that Jude was the one of whom Jesus had spoken in his letter. When Abgar heard this, he summoned Tobias before him and enquired about Tobias' new boarder, and asked Tobias to bring Jude to him at the palace. Tobias complied and early the following morning both Tobias and Jude were standing before King Abgar, who was still suffering from chronic pain in his joints.

As soon as the king gazed upon the face of Jude, he was transfixed by a vision and immediately fell to the ground to worship Jude. The king's attendants, who were scattered throughout the throne room, were immediately taken aback by the scene.

In their experience it had always been the visitors who would bow down before the king and not the other way around. They, of course, had not seen the divine vision that had been revealed to Abgar. Abgar opened his mouth and said, "Truly you are the disciple of Jesus, that Mighty One, the Son of God, who sent to me saying I will send you one of my disciples for healing and for life."

Jude explained that he had been sent to Abgar because of the faith that Abgar had in Jesus. He clarified further that this faith would produce that which he believed. Abgar let Jude know of his initial plans to bring his army against the Jews who opposed Jesus, but Jude reassured Abgar that God's will had been accomplished through Jesus' death and resurrection. Abgar then declared his faith in Jesus and in God the Father, before Jude.

With this declaration of faith, Jude placed his hands on the king, and the horrible disease that had afflicted him for so many years abated entirely. Jude, however, did not stop with the king, but also brought his servant Abdu forward placing his hands on him, thereby healing Abdu of his gout. Witnessing these miraculous cures in others as well as himself only served to bolster King Abgar's faith. So he humbly asked Jude if he would be willing to teach he and his people about the life and ministry of Jesus.

Jude politely explained to the king that although he had performed miraculous healings here in Edessa in Jesus' name, that his primary mission was the teaching and preaching of which Abgar spoke. So without further ado, Jude began to teach the Syrians in Edessa about Jesus and the basic credal affirmations about him in the early church.

In the palace itself, in addition to Abgar, he taught Abgar's mother, his wife, his sons, and many other nobles who frequented the palace. When Abgar attempted to pay Jude for his teaching, Jude promptly rebuked him, relating another episode from Jesus' life when he sent Jude along with sixty-nine other apostles out into the world. On that occasion Jesus had said to them, "Carry neither purse, nor scrip [archaic term for a bag carried by wayfarers], nor shoes…" (Luke 10:4). Jude further explained to Abgar that he and his fellow apostles had given away their possessions to enable them to serve Jesus unhindered. "How," Jude wondered, "could we then receive anything that is not ours?" Remembering this episode from his time with Jesus fondly reminded Jude of several parables he had taught them. He made sure to share with them the parable of the sheep and the goats and that of the narrow gate.

Having described Jesus' ministry on earth, including his death, resurrection and ascension, Jude then began to describe the continuing work of the apostles, who not only preached the gospel of Jesus, but healed the sick in Jesus' name, as he indeed had done in their presence with Abgar and his servant Abdu. One apostle in particular that Jude highlights in his retelling for his Syrian audience was Peter and his ministry in Rome.

He related a story involving Peter and James and their encounter with the wife of Claudius, the Emperor of Rome, which is only recorded in The Doctrine of Addai. The inhabitants of the palace were so pleased with Jude's preaching that Abgar asked Jude if he would preach to these things to the entire city. He then had Abdu, his servant, send a herald, who called for the entire city to assemble in the central square, called in Aramaic, 'the collapsed house,' *Beth-Thabara*.

This gave Jude the opportunity not to simply preach to the palace, but to all the inhabitants of the city. He preached with fervor explaining the life and ministry of Jesus with the basic creedal affirmations of the early church concerning him, as well as the healing power that had been granted to himself and the other apostles so that they might preach the gospel with authority. He called for them to repent and spoke of the future kingdom of God when the literacy rate would be one hundred percent so that every person would be able to read the divine record of their own deeds for which they would be called to account.

This talk of writing reminded Jude of the Mesopotamian god of writing Nebo (Akkadian Nabu), whose temple and image Jude had seen as he passed through the city. He, therefore, took this opportunity to address the issue of idol worship citing as examples, not only Nebo, but also Bel, an epitaph for Marduk in the Babylonian pantheon. He also spoke of a goddess Bath Nikal, which was one of many local names for Ishtar of Babylon, along with the goddess Taratha, also known as Atargatis. In this context, Jude also took aim at Arabian deities who are the objects of worship in Edessa, namely, the eagle, the sun, and the moon. He launched into the standard Jewish and Christian critique of idols found in Isaiah and the book of Acts that an item created with human hands should not then become the object of worship by the very one who created that item. This lead Jude from talking about the idols specifically to talking of the sacrifices and rites that the inhabitants of Edessa perform for these deities. Concerning these, Jude declared that they are not in fact sacrificing to gods, as they believe they are, but they are instead sacrificing to demons and devils.

When Jude finished preaching to the assembled crowd, his words were well received by all those who gathered to listen. Even a few reluctant souls eventually turned their hearts toward Christ. He then baptized the new believers. This greatly pleased Abgar, who commissioned Jude to build a church for his city in order that they might have a place to come to worship Jesus; as opposed to the idols, who had been the object of worship throughout the city. Then several of the chief priests of these pagan deities, who had now converted to Christianity, destroyed all of the altars throughout the city that they used to worship these pagan deities, with the sole exception of the great altar in the center of the city.

Jude appointed Aggai to act as the elder, Palut to act as the deacon, and Abshelama and Barsamya to act as scribes of this church in Edessa. He taught them the scriptures, which they studied intently and memorized. As the numbers of the church swelled, others took to building churches in the more remote parts of the city and Jude appointed priests to each of them.

In this way, word of Saint Jude, himself, and of the Christian gospel message more broadly, was being disseminated ever wider. Kings from surrounding areas sought the knowledge and miracles of Jude.

Saint Jude in the City of Amis

Based on the <u>Acts of Thaddaeus</u>, the legend of Saint Jude in the City of Amis gives us a glimpse into Jude's incredible ability to preach.

Before leaving Edessa, Jude promoted Aggai to the position of bishop of the region, Palut to the position of elder and Abshelama to the position of deacon. Believing that his work in Edessa was complete, Jude then travelled with a few of his own disciples to the city of Amis, in Mesopotamia along the Tigris River. As was his custom when he visited a city without an established church, Jude and his disciples had attended the synagogue service on the Sabbath to listen to the reading of the law. At the conclusion of the service, the high priest noticed this group of foreigners and questioned Jude as to the purpose of their visit. Jude seized upon this question as an opportunity to preach Jesus to the Jews in this city.

He presented the "bare bones" version of Jesus' life and ministry focusing mostly on Jesus' death and resurrection. He also described the ministry of the apostles and that as one of them, he had the power to drive out demons, to heal the sick and even to raise the dead. This word restored hope to many who heard it and they brought their sick and those possessed by demons to Jude and his disciples.

Not skipping a beat, Jude laid his hands on the sick, healing them and drove out the demons in the name of Christ from those who had been possessed. Once his healing ministry had drawn an audience, Jude then preached the gospel to those gathered round.

As a result of his preaching, many repented of their sins and were baptized. He stayed there for five years, built a church and appointed bishops, elders and deacons as he had at Edessa.

The End of an Incredible Life

As one can clearly see from the stories of Saint Jude, his life was incredibly important to the spread of Christianity. He converted sinners, healed the sick, and brought hope to people around the world. It is no wonder that we turn to such Saint Jude when we are need.

The various accounts of the death of Saint Jude seem to be as plentiful as the number of ancient sources. The Syriac Acts of Thaddaeus has Jude dying peacefully in Beiut on August 21st. According to the tenth century Menology of Basil II, Jude "headed for Arat, and there he was driven against a cross and stabbed with spears until he died."

According to the thirteenth century Armenian manuscript Le Synarxarion Armenien de Ter Israel, Saint Jude was ministering in Armenia when the King Sanatrouk threw him in a den of lions, because his daughter, Princess Sandoukht, had believed his teachings and followed Jude. Because of this she had become disobedient to her father, the king, causing him to put her to death. But the lions did not harm Jude, but only licked his feet. Sanatrouk then threw Jude into a furnace, but he did not burn. The king then had his executioners dispatch him with their swords, and this time they were successful.

While the exact account of Jude's passing is unclear, it is certain that his life and legacy lives on in the heart of Christians everywhere. The hopeless can find hope in the life of Saint Jude.

The Real Jude

The last two sections of this book provide an important context to the reader. After delving into the incredible life and legends of Saint Jude the Apostle, we must reflect on the sources that provide the story of his life.

To understand the complexity of the sources available about Jude the Apostle, it is important to acknowledge the multitude of names that appear in the various sources and the difficulty in determining which names refer to the same historical figure and which names refer to different historical figures. During this historical period individuals had given names, nicknames, and surnames. The multiple languages of the ancient sources only serve to complicate matters further.

The name of the writer of the epistle of Jude in Greek is Ἰούδας, which is translated into Latin as 'Judas' (Jude 1:1). This name belonged to at least three different figures in the New Testament period. The most notorious figure with this name was Judas Iscariot, who betrayed Jesus. This association caused later Christian writers to go to some extraordinary lengths to disambiguate more honorable individuals bearing this name from Judas Iscariot. The author of the Gospel of John identifies one "Judas...not the Iscariot" (John 14:22). English translators have chosen to disambiguate the author of the epistle from the despised disciple by writing the first name as a shortened form without a nominal ending, 'Jude' and the second as 'Judas'. Another Judas with the nickname Barsabbas is listed as an early Christian leader alongside Silas in the sequel to the Gospel of Luke (Acts 15:22).

The names become more complicated when one tries to collect information about Judas, the author of the epistle. In his letter, he identifies himself as "the brother of James" (Jude 1:1). When one looks for Judas, the brother of James, there is the parallel passage in the Gospels of Matthew and Mark where Jesus' Galilean neighbors ask rhetorical questions in which they identify members of Jesus' family whom they know personally.

Within this list appears "his brethren James and Joseph, and Simon, and Ἰούδας Jude" (Matt. 13:55; cp. Mark 6:3). Since James, the brother of Jesus, was a well-known apostle throughout the early Christian community, it would not be odd for the Jude in this list to identify himself in a letter as "the brother of James." The author of the Gospel of Luke actually uses this designation in his list of Jesus' twelve disciples, with the 11th disciple being "Ἰούδαν Jude the brother of James" (Luke 6:16). This disciple can then be further identified with the disciple named "Judas…not the Iscariot" who questioned Jesus in the Gospel of John (John 14:22).

After this point the names become even more complicated to sort out. There is no Judas, other than Iscariot, mentioned in the lists of the twelve disciples found in the Gospels of Matthew and Mark. In the Gospel of Mark, the place occupied by Judas, the brother of James, in Luke is filled by a disciple named 'Thaddaeus' (Mark 3:18).

As if the testimony was not already complicated enough, some of the ancient Greek and Latin manuscripts of Matthew contain an entirely different name altogether in this position, 'Lebbaeus'. Other ancient Greek and Latin manuscripts of Matthew contain the readings, "Thaddeus who is called Lebbaeus" and "Lebbaeus who is called Thaddaeus."

According to The Acts of Thaddaeus, the name Thaddaeus was not a given name, but rather a name given to this disciple at his baptism.

Then the issue of different languages comes into play (still with us?). In the Syriac language, which is a dialect of Aramaic spoken in the region of Syria where Jude is believed to have ministered, the name Addai appears in texts describing the same events where the Greek texts use the name Thaddaeus. Because Syriac does not have a distinct sound corresponding to Greek *theta*, the working hypothesis for many scholars is that the Syriac speakers simply did not pronounce it so that the Greek name Thaddaeus was pronounced Addai in Syriac. It should be noted that there are other scholars who think that the Syriac name Addai corresponds instead to the Greek names Adda, Addaios, or even Addai.

If reading this makes your head spin—you are not alone. The important take away here is that the New Testament itself has at least four different names that scholars connect with the man we know as

Saint Jude. Not all scholars agree in connecting all of these names with the same historical figure.

How We Know What We Know (The Sources)

In the previous sections, the gospel occurrences of this apostle were mentioned in detail. The gospels were all written in Greek and completed by the end of the first century A.D. The vast majority of the sources regarding the life of Saint Jude were written much later than the gospels. We leave it to the reader to determine what information should be taken as fact and what should be taken with a "grain of salt."

Aside from his status as a saint and an apostle, the Church has no official position on the authenticity and veracity of the later texts that describe the life of Saint Jude.

Pope Gelasius I (pope from 492-496 A.D.) did declare the letter from Jesus to Abgar apocryphal, and as such it should not be viewed as the words of Jesus directly. But beyond this, believers may decide for themselves which texts about Saint Jude they find compelling and uplifting to their faith and which they find problematic and untrustworthy.

The biography below has been written including all of the material available on Saint Jude without editorial judgment on their veracity.

After the gospel traditions, the first mention of Jude appears in the *Church History* written by Eusebius also in Greek during the fourth century A.D. But when he mentions the story of Abgar and Thaddaeus (Jude), he states that he is making a literal translation of a

Syriac text contained in the archives at Edessa itself. The text of Eusebius on this point reads as follows:

> Written evidence of these things is available, taken from the Record Office at Edessa, at that time the royal capital. In the public documents there, embracing early history and also the events of Abgar's time, this record is found preserved from then till now; and the most satisfactory course is to listen to the actual letters, which I have extracted from the archives and translated word for word from the Syriac as follows: (I 13.5)

Drijvers argues that this core tradition of the letter correspondence between Abgar and Jesus developed in the third century Syriac church as an orthodox response to the threat of Manicheism (H.J.W. Drijvers, "The Abgar Legend", In New Testament Apocrypha. Volume One: Gospels and Related Writings, 1991, 494-96). The founder of Manicheism, Mani, wrote six of his seven writings in Syriac, so this heresy would have been well-known to the Syriac speaking audience of this tradition.

Drijvers notes the following parallels between the two that led him to this conclusion. Addai (or Adda) was one of the most prominent missionaries of Mani. One of the Manicheans claims was that they possessed letters from Jesus. Just as Abgar called Jesus "the good physician," when he addressed King Shapur Mani said, "I am a physician from the land of Babylon." There is also the issue of the painted image of Jesus that is a prominent part of the legend. [Later texts describe the image as one 'not made by human hands', which is the variant used in the biography above.] In Manicheism, the portrait of Mani was set up on the altar and worshippers could receive forgiveness of sins from Mani by means of the portrait. These are the most obvious connections between this tradition and Manicheism.

Most of the later traditions maintain this core information connecting Abgar and Jude and then expand with further information. The Ethiopic text entitled <u>The Contending of the Apostles</u> is based on traditions that likely extend to the second century A.D. The work itself, however, is a translation of a Coptic work that likely dates to between 400-540 A.D. (E. A. W. Budge, <u>The Contendings of the Apostles. Vol. 1: Ethiopic Text</u>, 1899, VIII). The <u>Acts of Thaddaeus</u> is a Greek text written in the seventh century A.D. The <u>Apostolic History of Abdias</u> consists of a Latin collection of traditions concerning the apostles that dates from the sixth or seventh century A.D. The Italian church chronicler, the Blessed Jacobus de Vorgaine compiled <u>The Golden Legend</u> the in the thirteenth century A.D. The Armenian text <u>Le Synarxarion Armenien de Ter Israel</u> also date to the thirteenth century A.D.

Prayers to Saint Jude

Novena to Saint Jude

To Saint Jude, Holy Saint Jude, Apostle and Martyr, great in virtue and rich in miracles, near kinsman of Jesus Christ, faithful intercessor of all who invoke your special patronage in time of need. To you I have recourse from the depths of my heart and humbly beg to whom God has given such great power to come to my assistance. Help me in my present and urgent petition, in return I promise to make your name known and cause you to be invoked. Saint Jude, pray for us and all who invoke your aid. Amen

Prayer I

Most holy Apostle Saint Jude, faithful servant and friend of Jesus, the name of the traitor who delivered the beloved Master into the hands of His enemies has caused you to be forgotten by many, but the Church honors and invokes you universally as the patron of hopeless cases, of things almost despaired of. Pray for me, I am so helpless and alone. Make use I implore you, of that particular privilege given to you, to bring visible and speedy help, where help is almost despaired of. Come to my assistance in this great need, that I may receive the consolations and help of Heaven in all my necessities, tribulations and sufferings, particularly your request and that I may bless God with you and all the elect forever.

I promise, O blessed Saint Jude, to be ever mindful of this great favor, to always honor you as my special and powerful patron, and to gratefully encourage devotion to you. Amen.

Prayer II

Glorious Saint Jude, with faith in your goodness I ask your help today. As one of Christ's chosen Apostles, you are a pillar and foundation of His Church on earth. You are among the elders who stand always before God's throne.

Brother Jude, you are renowned for your kinship with Christ and your physical resemblance to our Savior. Help me remain close to Christ and resemble Him in my outlook and actions.

Holy Apostle, you are venerated for your work of preaching the gospel and your faithfulness to Christ by a martyr's death. Assist me to preach the good news of Christ by word and example, and remain steadfast in His service as you were.

From your place of glory, do not forget the needs and difficulties of Christ's little ones like me, still struggling on the way home to God. Pray for me that I may receive the consolation and help of heaven in my necessities, tribulations and sufferings, particularly (name special problem) and that I may praise God with you and all the elect forever.

Intercede for us all, gracious, brother Saint Jude, and pray for us to the Lord our God in our daily toil and our necessities. Amen.

Prayer III

O Glorious Saint Jude, you were honored to be a cousin as well as a follower of Jesus, and you wrote an Epistle in which you said: "Grow strong in your holy faith through prayer in the Holy Spirit." Obtain for us the grace of being people of faith and people of prayer. Let us be so attached to the three Divine Persons through faith and prayer on earth that we may be united with them in the glory of the beatific vision in heaven.

Prayer IV

Dear Apostle and Martyr for Christ, you left us an Epistle in the New Testament. With good reason many invoke you when illness is at a desperate stage. We now recommend to your kindness {name of ailing} who is in a critical condition. May the cure of this patient increase his/her faith and love for the Lord of Life, for the glory of our merciful God. Amen.

Prayer V

Glorious Apostle, Saint Jude Thaddeus, I salute you through the Sacred Heart of Jesus. Through His Heart I praise and thank God for all the graces he has bestowed upon you. I implore you, through His love to look upon me with compassion. Do not despise my poor prayer. Do not let my trust be confounded. God has granted to you the privilege of aiding mankind in the most desperate cases. Oh, come to my aid that I may praise the mercies of God. All my life I will be your grateful client until I can thank you in heaven. Amen.

Saint Jude, pray for us, and for all who invoke your aid.

Prayer VI

O most holy apostle, Saint Jude, faithful servant and friend of Jesus, the Church honoureth and invoketh thee universally, as the patron of hopeless cases, and of things almost despaired of. Pray for me, who am so miserable. Make use, I implore thee, of that particular privilege accorded to thee, to bring visible and speedy help where help was almost despaired of. Come to mine assistance in this great need, that I may receive the consolation and succor of Heaven in all my necessities, tribulations, and sufferings, particularly (here make your request) and that I may praise God with thee and all the elect throughout eternity. I promise thee, O blessed Jude, to be ever mindful of this great favour, to always honour thee as my special and powerful patron, and to gratefully encourage devotion to thee. Amen.

Prayer VII

May the Sacred Heart of Jesus be adored, glorified, loved and preserved now and forever. Sacred Heart of Jesus have mercy on us, Saint Jude worker of Miracles, pray for us, Saint Jude helper and keeper of the hopeless, pray for us, Thank you Saint Jude.

Made in the USA
Middletown, DE
11 July 2020